PRAISE FOR *CIPOTA*

Cipota is a brilliant collection of narrative poems that feel both new and familiar. Chelsea Guevara beautifully intertwines the personal and political with stunningly captivating words. The author uses figurative language as a paintbrush to create vivid images that the readers can grasp and hold on to. *Cipota* is gorgeously written and is a collection that everyone should read.

– Rudy Francisco, *Excuse Me As I Kiss the Sky*

'Cipota' means girl in Salvadoran Spanish, but Lord knows these poems are full-grown—delivered with the power of a woman determined to buck intergenerational curses and protect her most endangered kin. Few poets can dream of reaching Chelsea's natural charisma and vulnerability on the stage. With *Cipota*, Chelsea has earned one of the top spots in the current generation of Central American writers demanding our space and specificity not just in latinidad and poetry but the world.

– Willy Palomo, *Wake the Others*

Cipota marks the entrance of a bold new force in the Central American literary tradition: the fierce and necessary voice of Chelsea Guevara. This debut is an offering toward a better world, from a poet who knows the intricate, careful work of excavating memory. In these poems, Guevara embodies the incisive orature of the slam world alongside the meticulous storytelling in Salvadoran lineages. While Guevara's "Cumbia de los Salvadoreños" dances through the Salvadoran craft of survival, her poems offer us a full portrait of our humanity, inviting us to sing, cry, and heal along the way.

– Janel Pineda, *Lineage of Rain*

CIPOTA

CIPOTA

poems by
Chelsea Guevara

Button Publishing Inc.
Minneapolis
2025

CIPOTA
POETRY
AUTHOR: Chelsea Guevara
COVER DESIGN: Mel Nigro

ALL RIGHTS RESERVED

© 2025 by Chelsea Guevara

Published by Button Poetry
Minneapolis, MN 55418 | http://www.buttonpoetry.com

Manufactured in the United States of America
PRINT ISBN: 978-1-63834-135-2
EBOOK ISBN: 978-1-63834-129-1

First printing

CONTENTS

3   Part I: *Vanessa tiene otra mamá, pero nos llaman gemelas*
7   Part II: *still not fluent in Spanish (but I know all the bad words)*
8   los pajaritos
10 Cumbia de los salvadoreños
14 Soft
16 Hermana, ¿puedes hablar?
19 **Part III:** *somos artistas también*
20 ¡Ya viene la lluuuvia!
22 Dry
25 Like Rosaries
29 **Part IV:** *hogar es donde cantan los pájaros*
30 Mom is the First Metaphor I Learn For Water
32 All I Know
36 Las tías
37 Enzo
38 La Amor
40 Sweet Blood & Zancudos
45 **Part V:** *I think I've heard this story before*
46 Antepasadxs
49 Burn
53 In my dreams,
55 Pachita
59 **Part VI:** *I always cry when we leave Mamá Lupe's house*
60 Cipota (sin vergüenza)
62 Hija de todo lo sagrado
64 The Last Thing I Leave You With
65 Divine Protection
69 **Part VII:** *que contaré a los siguientes cipotes?*

73 **Acknowledgments**
75 **About the Author**
77 **Author Book Recommendations**
81 **Credits**

CIPOTA

PART 1

Vanessa tiene otra mamá, pero nos llaman gemelas

My sister didn't know I existed until I was two years old. I don't think papá knew how to tell her over the phone.

The first time we met, I was six. I only remember it in parts, as I do everything else. The road trip from Honduras is an endless curve I watch from my mother's lap. I eat cornflakes buried in powdered milk; face the open window to prevent the nausea from consuming my small body.

I never pay attention much on car rides; *una maña* I will never outgrow. Mom and papá laugh, they say I wouldn't know how to get home if they left me down the street and spun me around. Of course, if asked for an address, I could recite it. But I wouldn't know which direction to start walking in to get back to where we came from. All the houses fade into each other there…the same brown, beige, white. In El Salvador, everyone lives behind old pastels and rusty metal gates. Mamá Lupe's house shines turquoise, and none of the dishes match.

I am nudged into a room of strangers. This is the only memory of mine where my family members seemed *tall*. Vanessa's is the first face I see myself in; the resemblance that first made me think myself beautiful.

I wrap my arms around my sister for the first time and say nothing. The only words I know in Spanish are *cobija, pájaro, zapatos, hermana.* They must've taught me to say *I love you*, but I cannot remember. That's always the problem.

Vanessa
is studying to be a doctor,
just like papá did before he came to the states,
and I'm gonna be just like them.

Vanessa
drinks tequila and eats limones as a snack.
Teaches me how to salsa
and never yells.

Vanessa
wears crop tops,
has a hummingbird stretched across her rib cage,
and is the most perfect person I have ever known.

The only night I ever see her angry,
her uncle tells me that the more a man denies a child,
the deeper the resemblance carves her face–

tells me I look *just* like papá.

Vanessa says to ignore him,
and I do.
Vanessa es *igualita* a papá también.
and isn't she beautiful?

I watch her
carefully.
She doesn't smile with her teeth for the photo,
so neither do I;

they tell us we look like twins.

Daughters of different wombs
that share our father's face,

we are the feminine raised
as the first sons he wished for.
The daughters that still carry the family names
and put them on college degrees.

I don't know how long the moment lasted, but papá gently taps my arm to let her go. Reminds me there is an entire bloodline extending out to me, at this very moment, that I've only ever seen in pictures.

PART 11

still not fluent in Spanish (but I know all the bad words)

Somewhere over the border,
there is a song that plays uncensored on the car radio;
doesn't even cut out the word *puta*.
And my mouth falls open like it does
when I try to explain things in a language I know,
but my mouth has not learned yet.

LOS PAJARITOS

Mi amor,
when I tell you my ancestors are birds
I mean I watch from a distance.

I have never been able to get as close as I'd like.
My footsteps are too clumsy, always

have been. I take a step closer to look
and they are gone.

I strain to listen,
to find something in the warbles familiar
enough to translate because this

is how I've always learned about myself

through the mouths of others
who speak stories so holy,
they float

in a room
glittered with empty beer bottles,
with the primitos
tucked into the couch for an impromptu sleepover,
where a bocina
plays an old song about crossing the border,

this is where we've always learned about ourselves.

Mi amor,
when I tell you my ancestors are birds

I mean I try so hard to whistle like them;
cómo me enseñó mi papá.

And sometimes they do sing back,
remind me how often I've attempted the language
of someone I loved,
and not known what they were trying to tell me.

Please, let this count for something
because I do not know flight,
only weight. Only paper

airplanes folded sharp by my father's hands,
ones that go soft in my own,
too many creases to catch good air.

I know paper in water–
only a grasp of something I once knew,
but that no longer looks the same as it did.

Mi amor,
it is not ruined–
it is just different

and I have to remind myself of that.

Mi amor,
when I say my ancestors are birds

I mean my best dreams
have always been the ones
where I could fly.

CUMBIA DE LOS SALVADOREÑOS

if there's one thing I've learned from my dad
it's how to love cumbia   how to make a partner
out of the music so you never have to dance
by yourself   how to move your feet

until the heels don't hurt anymore and you forget
you're tired   my dad   taught me not to stutter

over the rhythm   but use my hips to speak
in música bachata   didn't even know he could spin

circles around me in zapateo hondureño
until my wedding

that night   the whole family moved
at the command of Hermanos Flores and Aniceto Molina

when I say my family loves to dance
I mean we *love* to dance
maybe because there is no sadness in dancing

I mean   because dancing is fun

when I say we love to dance
I mean we love to sing   too

and sure   we might sing sad songs
because en música latina there are a lot of sad songs
but *no*
salvadoreños don't get *sad*

turn up the music until we forget the lyrics
and speak in nothing but song notes

feel our lungs close tight like accordions
hold our breath until the tears
stop trying to make their debut   'cause

we aren't sad
no   we are just *good* actors

you know   I've only ever seen my tía cry once
and the men only cry when they're drinking
turn up the music

we don't sound like this 'cause we're actually sad
the break in our voice as we sing back to Vicente
is us just playing the part
really using our imagination

I mean   primo
imagine being heartbroken?

imagine   being so weak   that you had to sing
this song to heal yourself in all the ways
you couldn't alone?

isn't that fucking *wild*?
to be so human it hurts?
to be so hurt someone else actually sees?

naaaambre,   not us!
¡porque somos salvadoreños!

remember   primo?
all the late drinking nights we spent listening to war stories
from our fathers' childhoods?

we are collections   of everything they did to survive
monuments they built of their tough skin
and gifted a much better life.

what else can we be *except* invincible?

when the older generation carries this much trauma
it becomes the kind of heavy
that leaves no room in the family tree for weak limbs
but sometimes

when I hear my dad's stories about home   sadness
becomes the scariest thing I need to learn how to feel
more frightening than my anger ever has been

I find myself wailing to the tune of all the pain
my parents and theirs had to live through
left grieving for the childhoods they never knew
but gave to me

those are their stories though   not mine
I mean   I would never need anything for my mental health
'cause I'm built like them
I mean   I went to three therapy sessions and then stopped
'cause I felt guilty
I mean   I'm just too busy
I mean   I'm just not sad enough to need it
it's just not in our DNA

don't you know?

Salvadoreños know how to survive
put on cumbia   and sing along
the tears you see falling are not for us
they are the only payment that guitar strings will accept
so we're just playing the part

Salvadoreños know how to survive
to never expect a thing of this world
and figure out how to help ourselves

what kind of Salvadoreña would I be
if I couldn't?

I mean   primo

who am I on the days that I can't?

SOFT

Moni comes over to write poems,
and instead we talk for hours.

Take turns at the dining room table, crying
over the things we don't want to tell our mothers,
and can't tell anyone else.

And then we move on,
pick a poem from our drafts about anything
that doesn't make us feel this much.

I've always wished to be softer.
To know how to paint my nails tidy,
sing sweet things, like indie love songs,
and keep good posture

but I always get polish on the skin.
Pick until I bleed
and I was taught to scream well before I could sing.

I am the messy girl,
with a bad, bent back
and furrowed brows

Once,
during kickboxing practice
my best friend kicked my jaw off its hinges;
left it a creaky, unstable door
and I've never spoken confidently since.

I wonder what would've happened if I stayed in ballet;
learned how to do a pirouette instead of how to throw a punch.

I wonder if I would still carry my parents' strong character
and bad temper.

Wonder
if I would still know how to guard myself
with my mother's wild tongue;
my father's stone face.

Wonder
if I could be softer,
and still survive.

HERMANA, ¿PUEDES HABLAR?

I call Vanessa from the bathroom at work

'cause papá found out about my first boyfriend at 16.
Just like he found out about her first boyfriend at 16,
and he's no less angry now.

I tell her that he asked me what I liked about him so much,
and I told him that he's funny.

Me preguntó si iba ser payaso para pagar las facturas o qué
si chistoso sería suficiente

y le dije que no
pero que le amaba
y eso sí sería suficiente.

PART III

somos artistas también

Somewhere over the border,
there is art
wrapped around the body of every brick wall
stone dressed in spray-paint

and there are artesanías in La Palma
and there are poetry nights in San Salvador
and there are murals of San Romero everywhere
and there is art
and there is art
and there is poetry
and there are poets

I didn't know there was art.

It gets lost in my family's stories
about the farm and the war. It gets lost
in the wide-open mouths of politicians

talking about shithole countries.

In all the talk of pandillas, y la violencia, and survival,
they don't talk about how smart we are,

from the books we've held,
or the ones we couldn't afford.

They don't talk about all the beautiful things
we make with our hands.

¡YA VIENE LA LLUUUVIA!

The first time I fell in love with the rain,
papá and I sat huddled together beneath a toy umbrella.
Listened to the storm through pink plastic on the porch
in a neighborhood new to us both.

Everyone says papá looks really mean. If you ask my mother about the first time they met, this is what she knew of him before his name. But he stretches his arm out the front door; palm up and open to the promise of gray clouds. And he smiles. We don't have a real umbrella; there's not much need for one in the desert. But today it rains, so papá and I run to pull a flimsy replica out of my room.

Here, everyone has questions I don't know how to answer. They ask me what I am, not who. Everyone just wants to know why my face looks like that. Why the pale girl has dark colochos. I tell people I was born in El Salvador. This is the first lie I offer to the world. The only one that never makes me feel guilty; like it could almost be true.

Papá is the best storyteller I know

pulls el pulgarcito with him across borders,
and builds us a sanctuary in the dry heat.

Papá always knows when the fruit is ready,
shows me how to gut the papaya.

Papá drives me and my brother to the mountains,
teaches us how to angle the weight of the machete.

Papá hates big crowds,
but dances with me to all the cumbias they play at the quince.

Papá doesn't read poetry,
but explains each Vicente song he's dedicated to a person he loves.

When I finally learn to tell people about where I'm from, it is because

Papá teaches me how to whistle,
and the memories flutter out of my mouth like hunted doves.
Like pet parrots.
Like split tailed-torogoces.

I didn't understand exactly why he wanted to go outside in that kind of weather, and I didn't ask. It rained, and suddenly I understood how much there is to learn from his silence.

Years later, I am in the homeland for the first time by myself. It's August. And every single day, for the entire month, Mamá Lupe says, "¡Ya viene la lluuuvia!" I open the door, step beneath the storm, and listen. When I go inside, it's only to call papá.

DRY

we are nothing to you
but a series of spilt lineages.
bodies of bloody wounds,
so you come like hounds

thirsty for another blood-stained story.
demand we sink our nails into scars,
revive them so you can drink.

you are
the driest swallow.
the sharpest tongue that spits centuries-old sawdust,
and I almost choke when you ask me

what are you?
salvadoran?
tell me about the gangs,
the murder capital,
the most dangerous country in the world

i say no.

i will not tell you about the destruction
so you can lick your dry lips over it.

all you claim to know of us is the "discovery"
is the story de los conquistadores who looked a lot like you
who looked a lot like *God*

you say foreign aid
military investment
Democracy

cough up blood from a dry throat

say free market,
development,
Capitalism

you say solution,
savior,

but you never say *Genocide*.

ask us instead about the wars that chased our families here
la tierra left manchada by foreign weapons
and brown boys dying for your imperialist conquest.

you don't ask about me,
just the violence you name me descendant of.
you would never know

but i am a central american scholar.
which means
every time i open a textbook,
i learn of a new loss.

but i am also a poet.
which means
every time i open a notebook,
i find another memory i mourned
before i learned the words to describe it.

oh how some days,
soy la académica triste más triste del mundo.
oh how some days,
i am still the small girl listening to her father's stories;
his voice
stiff as sugarcane.

we spend a lifetime
tending to the wounds we inherit with our parents' memories

and you beg to see them bleed,
desperate to quench the thirst of a conquest you deny knowing

but blood
is salty.
could never cure a man in drought.

yet we are still stuck here
in the same positions–

You
demanding what you feel is owed:
a story

about the death of a people
to make you feel alive.

us
with nothing
but a heartache the size of a homeland,
the scars of a native tongue severed,
the grief of a history we still have to dig for
under bodies
you'll never ask the names of.

LIKE ROSARIES

On the week I have to give my final decision to each graduate school, I carry Cenizas *by Cynthia Guardado, and* Lineage of Rain *by Janel Pineda, with me like rosaries.*

I pull *Cenizas* out of my bag in the dark;
set it on my pillow to read in the morning.

> we are just
> small girls
> sifting through the remnants of memories
> as touchy as volcanoes
>
> careful,
> like you can still feel the heat;
> like it still burns you.
>
> crying
> is something you are still learning to do
> without self-loathing.
>
> and this book makes you do a lot of it.
>
> in a rough draft somewhere,
> you compare your tears to rainwater
> or a river
> or the muddy puddles
> at the curbs of the colonia.
>
> how beautiful you describe something, bicha,
> that you always thought had made you ugly
>
> *and you have always loved the water.*

I wake up with *Lineage of Rain* next to me,
and realize I had no bad dreams that night.

I hold both in my hands;
grateful to be reminded I'm not alone
despite how long the world convinced me I was.

PART IV

hogar es donde cantan los pájaros

Somewhere over the border,
there are hundreds of birds singing outside the airport
asking me not to leave.

And my lips tug for a smile, open
and wait for a language I know

but my mouth has not learned yet.

How do I tell the birds
we never wanted to go in the first place?

MOM IS THE FIRST METAPHOR I LEARN FOR WATER

It takes Mom and I two whole days, backs bent over Mr. Clean and rubber gloves, to sift through the apartment. Nana's husband passed away, and we spend most of the time all saying sorry to each other for the things we could not control. I wonder when I first recognized apology as kinship between women. The weight of any one person's grief split between our hands; a condolence constantly squirming up the back of the throat.

Guilt is a houseguest I am learning to ask to move out. Trying to not say sorry again, because I've already said it too many times, is a practice in biting the tongue; muscle split and bleeding between enamel. I don't know why asking for forgiveness feels like a requisite for speaking, but

I always apologize when I talk
too much or at all.
Have a habit of treating my voice like loose change,
mortified by the way it sounds,
like it was an accident I even made a noise at all but

Mom collects all my writing.
Is my first audience,
the first reader I cobble a book together for,
the first person who thought my work was good enough to make me share it.

Mom's voice moves like lightning,
like it could silence a whole city.
Command everyone's attention
with or without starting a fire.

Everyone says I look like papá, but
Mom teaches me to let my voice bloom like thunder,
to crack the silence the world expects of us,
and the resemblance becomes undeniable.

Hours before the plane ride back, Mom and I stare at the water seeping through cuffed pant legs. Salt stinging shaved legs, sand consuming our feet like an offering at an altar. She tells me she wasn't convinced about papá's choice for my name until she realized it would hold the sea; a cleanse of salt. Mom is the first metaphor I learn for water.

ALL I KNOW

1. I laid in the grass, and I only checked for stains twice.
2. I sat hunched on the sofa, and I stopped pulling at the hem of my shirt.
3. I said what I wanted to say,

and I did not apologize for sounding dumb.

And I did not   and I did not   and I did not
think myself dumb,   think my body ugly,   think

about how everyone might speak
of the girl with green manchas on her clothing

and is this not   and am I not
                         beautiful?

                         for once?

I do not think so hard about myself

                         I splinter.
So many scars on my hands,
                         I cannot find
mis huellas   my way
                            back
                            home

                            home
                  is a lucid dream.
      Somethingabouthumidityisalwaysfamiliarbut
          sayingitoutloudmakesitsoundabsurd
               allIknowissaltbutnotsea.
allIdreamofisrainbutIwakeawitheredthingineverywinterssnow

here, everything looks the same
and I do not belong

                                        here,
                        everything looks familiar,
                          and I ask to stay longer

like if I do,
                a memory I once loved
will come back to me
like it never   left;
like it would fix everything.

                        I do not know
                         where I am
                        and I do not know
                         who I am–

                        all I know is

there are no better frutas than the ones picked
by my father's hands.

He raps his knuckles
on the rind of the   sandia,
puts his ear close,
and listens for it to echo back
in the language of ripe moment;
holds the mangos
in the pressure of his palms

I wish to one day skin a   papaya
as close to the   flesh
as he does

swing a   machete
and cut through
the branch of a tree like   jícama.

At a   time,
where my sister and I still
cannot say all that we need to
in each other's languages
she bathes los   jocotes in alguashte;
shows me how to leave

only the seeds behind   seeded lychas,
prickled shells torn in two.

Mamá Lupe holds a bag of lychas
teaches me to ask for what I need
in a tongue that will one day help me tell the truth.

All I know are stories,
and I'm trying to remember them correctly.
All we know is love,
but their god in this   desert
has never known us.

All my dreams,
rest on the premise of   flight
or escape, meaning all my   joy
has never known
an existence without   fear;
calls out his name
with her first breath.

I am always a   mouthful,
a stutter of teeth
and you teach me to sing
and I am terrified

of doing something I haven't learned to do well yet,
of being asked to translate and having to admit
I don't understand it all either.
of being asked for proof
and fluttering like faulty   memory

I cut a mango before bed. I cannot peel with the blade well enough not to waste it, but I cut the fruit in four and barely shave the semilla. And my father recalls the crowds of mango trees they plucked from as children. And I tell him, "I want to see them one day." And he tells me, "They do not exist as before." And I think

we must be lost   *we are still searching*

in the distance between fronteras,
in the stretch of the diaspora,
in the gaps of conversations,
trying to find a way with words
a way to each other
a way back   home.

LAS TÍAS

Lately,
everyone keeps asking me
how much weight I've gained since the wedding,
keeps reminding me how beautiful
I used to be

pero las tías me dicen "Ay que *chula*"

y hay momentitos
where I believe them.

ENZO

The year I move away from home, my little brother goes through his first heartbreak at 14. He spends the phone call mourning all his favorite songs; each one dedicated to her. He tells me he can't listen to them anymore. And I tell him one day he will; eventually the memories stop hurting. At least, I think most do.

A month later, my husband asks me for a divorce on our seven-year anniversary *exactly*. Like chapter slammed close. Like clean break through bone. Like scream without an echo. And every song in my headphones is a swallowed cry. A memory I can't figure out how to lay to rest.

When I called my mother, I could not stop crying.
When I called my father, I did not cry at all.
When I called my little brother, I apologized.

Enzo was born to two sisters. My ex was the closest thing he had to a brother for a long time. I lie, tell him I'm okay, and he asks me no questions in the silence after. Just plays me the same, slow love song he's been practicing on the ukulele. The saddest strings that pull all the grief back to me at once. He's learned the lyrics since January. Since I told him he was going to be okay. I mute myself until the song's over.

LA AMOR

You tell me
you do not know if you love me anymore.
And I know
that you do not love me anymore.

I spend the day
thinking about how many times
I've known a man who does not love a good woman
but does not let her go

I spend the day
thinking about how since we were kids, I told you,
I've always *hated* the cold.
Hated the way even the bones shake against the skin,
beg the body to give them more than what it has been

but I also told you
that I'd rather be alone,
rather tremble between goosebumps
than beg for the warmth of a man who once loved me
who does not love me anymore
but does not let me go.

Anger has always been the easiest weapon in reach,
the machete I keep by my bedside,
the only way I know how to protect the people I love

and between the two of us,
I wield it against myself.

Wonder if I am the good woman I speak of.
Wonder what would have happened
if I could've been better.

But Moni and Sammi answer every message.
My mother cries with me,
and says a prayer over the phone.
Melissa is a state away,
but sends me her love and a late-night box of cookies.
April reminds me that love
is not indecisive,
does not have to be reminded of your worth.
Brenda makes me tea in her kitchen
and tells me the walls are thin here–
hardly adequate for a breakdown, but I can still scream if I need to.
Daniella calls me powerful
when all I can mold are apologies from shaky breath

and I know,
in a life
where I deserve
this kind of love
from these kind of women

I deserve much more
than a lukewarm love
from you.

SWEET BLOOD & ZANCUDOS

América tells me that the zancudos eat me alive
because my blood is sweet
that's what her mami always says

and I admit that though,
I'd like to believe myself a stone-cold bitch,
my heart churns like wet cement,
burns
sticky and slow. I admit to being a lover girl

how embarrassing

to have a heart so soft
even the mosquitos know they can take from you.

In Oaxaca,
I tell the girls all about the divorce
and they ask me if I'm okay
and of course I say yes

I do not tell them
that most days I believe I will never be loved again.

Instead, I admit I wish for a love
that spreads like a swallow of honey
that you can still feel in your body
long after the first spoonful.

Did you know
it is the one bottle in your kitchen that can never expire?

I wish for a love
that blushes pink.
Warms the body like the last touch
before you leave your lover–
even when the *costumbre* threatens to kill all the color in your cheeks.

I wish for a love
that burns heavy; a shot of aguardiente
pressed from sugarcane

the kind of sweet you can still taste
even in the recoil
the kind that still makes you go back for more
every time.

PART V

I feel like I've heard this story before

Somewhere over the border,
I am convinced that I know more than the body allows me to.

There are memories as fuzzy
as cattails that have grown
over centuries calling me back
to this land. Ones that, if I grab
too hard, will turn seedling fluff
and fall through my fingers.
Ones that I know,
but my mouth has not learned yet.

ANTEPASADXS

White teacher asks me if my family from El Salvador is rich
or something, demands to know if this is why I do not have poems

to pull out of the indigenous parts of myself. And the anger
makes me so sick that I'm silent. And the guilt is so real

that it must be mine. The whole day, I think about how tío Carlos
was bottle-fed coffee because they could not afford cow's milk.

And God bless my grandmother's body that could not produce enough
to feed her first son. The guilt must have been so heavy, I wonder

if it ever left. It's always the hardest to forgive yourself for the things
you cannot do. But I tried. Asked my father, the best historian

of our family's blood, what he knew about the Nawat people
in our lineage, how much presence they have in a heritage

we've always called home. He told me we don't count by percentages.
We are whole.

Angry, white teacher asks me if my family from El Salvador is rich
or something. If this is why I will not write the poem he wants

for a competition, and isn't it funny? How history repeats itself?
Another white man discovers the ways in which he can take

a brown girl and make her useful to him. Breaks her people's sad history
down to numerical values, and waits for her to write a piece

people will congratulate *him* for. Tells her she's a true artist, a storyteller,
but only if the white people in the audience can relate to it.

Reminds her she is worth nothing
unless he says so
unless he edits the piece first
unless he approves it as the proper angry-brown-girl-poem
their public allyship can handle.

How could he make me feel guilty for not knowing enough
about the indigenous parts of myself? Of our people?

When the world does so much to hide these memories
and then convince us that they are too far back

to be worth anything? When the real story is so painful
your DNA deja vus. Your chest aches

from learning something you've always needed to know–
from learning something you should've known already.

It's always the hardest to forgive yourself for the things you cannot do.

This poem
is an apology to my ancestors or
a conversation.

I'm unsure how much you blame me
for not knowing the things trampled beneath Catholic crosses
and American bootstraps

or if you know that the guilt is so heavy,
I wonder if it will ever leave.

*Perdóname, pensé que a aprender el español, regresaría a mis raíces
cuando en realidad,*
I only traded one colonizer's language for another.

Forgive me, for not looking for you sooner.
I've been playing a game of telephone
passed down for centuries.

An oral history like a whisper of static,
if we remember to pick up the phone at all.

But I promise,
I'm trying to remember
to find the ways you are here.

I look for you in mirrors

draw a map between my face,
and my father's,
and yours.

Start from our nariz chata,
to the hairline that grows waves the color of coffee,
to the one scar I have on my forehead,
to the many my father holds deep between his pores.

Forgive me for not being able to apologize in your tongue.
Perdóname, por no saber sus nombres.

It does not mean I will never learn.

BURN

We come from homelands
stuck in fever.

From nations
grounded in the heat of volcanoes,
grown beneath a scorching sun.

We've got bodies
built to sweat through a swell,
but never break.

We know survival, even
in suffocating heat.

We beam about all the things
we can survive without
saying a word, how close we can be
to the sun without burning up.

But I've heard them

misspeak a wildfire,
and call it a sun.
I've seen a mother
mistake her son for a star

and when it happens,
the smoke is always louder than the whispers,
but they all tell his origin story the same way.

He was the first born–
the first flicker in the womb
of a woman always known to be full of light,
and she had to leave him,

her child,
just a small flame in the house of her mother,
and the guilt consumed her.

By the time she saw him again,
he had blown up,
turned incendio

but all she saw
was light.
All she felt
was a glow she'd been missing

and because of it,
they let him burn up the whole goddamn house-

blamed everything but him for the destruction
when it all went up in flames.

Said

it's all these drugs
a combustion of chemicals-
it's not *him*,
it's the gasoline that makes him this way-
that makes burn victims out of the girls

but is he not
light?
Is he not
what her world revolves around?

So they all pray for him,
or to him-
worship him like the sun
they believe him to be,
and forget the daughters in the process.

We are taught to believe men
the saints of storybooks

like the Bible

watch them scorch the whole sky
and teach the women,
long before they're women,
not to talk about the weather,

that the heat is never as bad as they say it is,

but still teach the women,
long before they're women,
that the dark
is not the only thing they need to be afraid of.

I can never look at a candle in church the same way again.
We all know an inferno that once resembled a simple flame.

A man who shapeshifts into conflagration over
and over,
but they never put him out.

Instead, they say this girl,
like the last,
got too close to the flames
and *goddamn it!*

Didn't we tell her what could happen
if too much skin was exposed?
Didn't we tell her
how flammable she was?

We've spent generations making sure no one sees us sweat,
then spend another one
choking on smoke,
watching another wildfire leave the world charred
only to deny that anything is burning,

to let him close to the babies
and pretend every breath in
is not a danger to the body,

to lie about what he's done,
and pretend that this
is another thing we can survive
without saying a word.

The ones with all the answers
act like they don't know how to heal a burn.
And it is the coldest realization to find that they don't,

that they refuse to recognize a blistered body
because it is too much
like looking in a mirror.

They were only ever taught how to hide the injury,
how to trap the heat under the skin
and watch how it festers into a family's lineage,

watch how the women
get stuck in swell for so long,
this silence becomes a fever no one ever learns how to break.
And so they expect us
to forget the abuse,
and get together on Sundays.
On Christmas.

On any other holy day they demand us to forgive,
but never teach the men to repent,

watch the sun
commit his sins,
and watch the daughters
burn.

IN MY DREAMS,

the apartment is so cramped it's suffocating.
But I look around

and it's just   you and me   crowded by empty space.

You are staring at me from across the room
like you always did.
I say, "I love you,"
and suddenly
I am crying in front of a stranger.

There are no divorce papers on the counter.
No Polaroids collecting dust in my desk drawer.
No veil hidden in the back of my closet.
No wedding dress thrown in the dumpster.

Generational curses wear the skin of cockroaches here.
I squash the last one beneath my father's chancleta
and suddenly hundreds more pop through the floorboards.
You are still
staring at me from across the room

so I leave,

return to the places where I have always been loved.

Papá Nay sits in the same spot outside the kitchen door,
and tells me a story about my father.
I speak to him in the only language he ever knew,
and I never have to grieve a lost conversation.

Grampa meets me at the point of the mountain,
and tells me a story about my mother.
I ask him all the right questions about the only place they've ever called
home, and I never have to wonder how well I remember him.

I wrap myself completely in a hamaca-

like all the primitas did before we became tías
before we became wives
before they stopped calling us cipotas-

and emerge a cloud of green feathers.

All their voices,
all my poems,
are preserved in every flap of wings.
My name
becomes whatever song the birds sing-

wherever you go after,
you spend every morning searching for me in the sky.

Wherever I go after,
I am free.

PACHITA

sometimes, you need to grieve–
there are too many stories to keep in.
sometimes, you need to grieve–
your tíos will recount them differently.
sometimes, you need to grieve–
you will be too young to understand why but
unbury all the versions.
Jarred seashells dug from wet sand,
eventually you will have collected enough
to make sense of why you kept them in the first place.

sometimes, you need to grieve what you've lost–
fear will be the only face you recognize.
sometimes, you need to grieve what you've lost–
it's what keeps you alive.
sometimes, you need to grieve what you've lost–
it might try to drown you but
papi will teach you how to swim.
Mom will show you how to love the sea she named you for.

sometimes, you need to grieve what you've lost before you–
nightmares of memories you never made will bare their teeth.
sometimes, you need to grieve what you've lost before you–
mornings will be a frantic search for phantom bites on the body.
sometimes, you need to grieve what you've lost before you–
you will grow up but
still be uneasy around chuchos.
Papi will hate when you and the primos come home after dark.

Sometimes, you need to grieve what you've lost before you can name it.
The men in your family will love songs that make you cry when alone.
Sometimes, you need to grieve what you've lost before you can name it.
You'll raise your glass to the chorus you can never remember completely.
Sometimes, you need to grieve what you've lost before you can name it.

Nostalgia will forever be a low-tide around your ankles,
heart held together like a sandcastle,
always cracked open on the shore of somewhere new you found home in.
You will never have the right words for goodbye.

Sometimes, you need to grieve what you've lost before you can name it.

PART VI

I always cry when we leave Mamá Lupe's house

Somewhere over the border,
after the plane ride back,

my father eats Pollo Campero con ketchup like we do at home,
and I eat frozen tamales after unpacking the suitcases.
My grandmother sends me a bag of crema,
and it's enough to draw the joy out of hiding,

even if it's diluted,
drowning in all of the longing in my body for a country that is home
but has never been *my* home.

Because somewhere over the border,
sometimes,
feels like no home at all.

Because somewhere over the border,
I have to explain that El Salvador is not in Mexico,
explain why my accent doesn't sound like a direct import.
I am waiting for my mouth to catch up-
to learn the language of my father that I swear
begs me to remember something that I know is there

but I have not found yet.

CIPOTA (SIN VERGÜENZA)

you leave home,
and it will be
the greatest (most selfish) thing you've ever done.

Which is to say,
the greatest (most selfish) thing you can do
is choose yourself (again).

Janel told you
this is a decision you must make on your own
so you did (and you thought of them the whole time).

When you called your family to tell them,
(you wished) he was proud of you-

(you imagined what it would be like if) pride in the daughter was born
from the moments she gripped independence between knuckles
so strained, she'd fight anyone for it (even her father?)
like they taught her to (even her father).

(What about) the family?
You, (selfish) girl,
(how could you) make a life for yourself—

we always wanted you to study (medicine, or science, or math).
We always wanted you to do something (we didn't have the opportunity to do ourselves).
We always wanted you to be someone (who made good money).
We always wanted you to not suffer (the way we had to).

¿Te recuerdas de las historias que tu papá te contó de su niñez?
You've always wished to be so smart (and you are).
You've always wished to make him proud (and you do).
You've always wished to be like him (he, too, disappointed his father once).
You've always wished to be like him (he left home, too).
You've always wished to be like him (and you are).

HIJA DE TODO LO SAGRADO

I am the flame my mother whispered into woman,
the steel my father sharpened into machete.

I am the masa my tías shape into sustenance,
the hands that make the harvest holy.

I am the clap of my grandmother's command,
small body of thunder.

I am the volcano collapsed into caldera,
the eruption and the rain.

I am all that came before me,
and all that came before me is powerful.

I am my last name's rebellion,
a miracle born out of a church's rejection.

I am the memory found at the bottom of the bottle,
the story revived in ranchera.

I am the regrowth after the drought,
the soil that remembered all she gives life to.

How dare you ever
make me think myself less than mountain?
Press your ear to my veins, love,
can't you hear the rivers?

I am the tide the moon calls for,
the pull of the sky.

I am the constellation you proposed to me under,
but you forgot my name

forgot to look for me
when the world got bigger.

Did you see me there?
In the shine of her silver?

Did my touch stain her hands
when she traced your tattoos?

Breathe in now, love—
does the temperature of our last kiss chill you, too?

Does the heat of cumbias
bring you my memory in heartburn?

When she says your name,
does my accent burst through your memories like a broken dam?
Does the nostalgia almost drown you?

I am the daughter of all that is sacred,
blasphemous to be the wife of a non-believer.

I am the feminine that carries her family's legacy,
bless that I die to the same name I was born with.

I am the woman I've always wished to be,
the only lover I need.

I am the love that I can only explain in translations,
in songs my parents played when I was young

I am the healing pressed into paper,
all the poems I write ~~you~~.

THE LAST THING I LEAVE YOU WITH

refrain from "I Wish You Roses" by Kali Uchis

You wished me a loneliness that stretched like drought
a heartbreak that stung, dry lips
a dehydration that lasted;
at least longer than yours.

I wish you roses

and I wish you honey
and I wish you sugar cane
and I wish you aguardiente

and I wish you all the love
we couldn't find in our kitchen.

DIVINE PROTECTION

Un billete de dos dólares en la cartera

pa' que nunca se te quede vacía.

El corazón crudo de un colibrí

pa' que tu puntería nunca falle a las palomas.

A hop to avoid the escoba from sweeping my feet;

I want to get married someday.

A sign of the cross from your grandfather's hands

pa' que todos lleguen seguros a Utah.

Un rosario, siempre cerca de la puerta principal

so no matter where you go, God will protect you.

Unas artesanías on the kitchen walls

so missing home doesn't hurt so much.

PART VII

que contaré a los siguientes cipotes?

Somewhere over the border,
I imagine having children

and how I wonder
if they would inherit this distant remembering,

and how I hope
it wouldn't hurt as much–

but that I'll tell them a story,
and they'll feel the same gnaw in their chest;
search for something in a hollow jaw.
And I'll tell them,
"You *knew* what you were just thinking.
You *knew* what you were just about to say—

take as much time as you need

it will come back to us.

It will come back."

button poetry

ACKNOWLEDGMENTS

To the whole team at Button Poetry, I cannot thank you enough for all the time and care you've dedicated to this collection, for your belief in my work, for holding this book throughout the publishing process as softly as I did.

To my family, all the poems, all the stories, all the words in the world could not describe the gratitude I have for you. Mom, thank you for forever being my biggest fan, the first audience to my writing, the first person that saw my work as something worth sharing. Papá, you are the greatest storyteller I know; the reason why I am a poet. Mil gracias por compartir su vida conmigo, y por enseñarme que cualquier cosa que pasa en la vida nunca sería más fuerte que nosotros. A Vanessa y Enzo, thank you for loving me and supporting me in ways that make me kinder to myself, and for hyping me up in my artistic dreams. A mi Mamá Lupe, gracias por las horas que me ha contado sobre los milagros de nuestra familia, por recordarme que Dios siempre está conmigo. A mi tía Ceci, gracias por recordarme de mi poder como mujer en este mundo, por recordarme pensar en lo bonito que nos espera mañana.

To the Kearns High School Slam team, thank you. Your softness and honesty has made me a better person and a better poet. To Dra. Gema Guevara, thank you for providing me with the first tools and guidance necessary to better understand my family's place in a complicated history. Because of your classes, I found the words and the confidence to tell the world about it.

To Willy, mi hermana, you are the first person I go to when I'm doubtful of what I've written. Thank you for protecting me as you push me. You radicalized me into believing in myself, into leaning into the want of a better world, and letting that desire guide me in my journey. Monica and Sammi, mis maripositas, my first poetry peers, thank you for all the hours yapping and workshopping you've gifted me. To my plumitas de la colectiva, the growth this book required of me to be created would not have been possible without your friendship, love, and guidance. To all my friends who became healers during the most challenging year of my life, thank you for putting me back together again and again. Out of that labor of love, I had the strength to keep pushing forward in order to make this possible. Thank you. I love you.

When I say that there are too many people to thank for *Cipota*, it's because I've been impacted by too many poets to count over the years. Every poet I have the honor of knowing has contributed to my immense growth as a writer and person. To all the amazing womxn I've had the honor to share space with at the Womxn of the World Poetry festivals over the years, thank you for your presence, for your power, for your poems that inspired me to believe in bigger for myself.

This book only exists because of the immense amount of love I'm blessed to know in this lifetime. This book only exists because of all of you, and I'm eternally grateful.

All my love,

Chelsea Elisandra Guevara

ABOUT THE AUTHOR

Chelsea Guevara is a U.S.-Salvadorian poet from Salt Lake City, Utah. In 2024, she won the Womxn of the World International Poetry Slam, becoming the first Salvadoran and the first Utahn to earn a national individual slam title. Currently a student in the University of Arizona's Latin American Studies graduate program, she utilizes her academic research to inform her creative work centering culture, history, memory, and identity. Chelsea's microchapbook *Somewhere Over the Border* was a finalist for the Gunpowder Press Alta California Chapbook Prize in 2023. You can find her work on Button Poetry, *Write About Now Poetry*, and *Mapping Literary Utah*.

AUTHOR BOOK RECOMMENDATIONS

crown noble by Bianca Phipps

With stories spun delicate and strong, *crown noble* serves as witness to the toll of relationships, what they demand of our individuality, and proves the frailness of generational silence when confronted by a single voice. Bianca's poems wrestle with love's complexities in an honest recognition of the hurt, and a reclamation of all the small parts of life that soften the wounds. *crown noble* shows that despite the fear, the mess, the grief it sparks, love continues to drive us.

BloodFresh by Ebony Stewart

BloodFresh is an altar to truth and to hurt; a place for both celebration and grief to gather. Through poems that grapple with both internal and external battles, Ebony proves joy to be the most divine and powerful weapon of resistance. An intimate reflection on the cost that accompanies healing and growth, *BloodFresh* leaves the reader with a burning chest, and the overwhelming belief in all the good there is and is to come.

CREDITS

Assistant Editors
Reese Brunette
Corbin Kimrey
Rabi Michael-Crushshon
Isabelle Miller
Sarah Tachau
Alix Wolf

Book Photography
Emily Van Cook

Cover and Interior Design
Charley Eatchel
Mel Nigro

Distribution
SCB Distributors

Ebook Production
Siva Ram Maganti

Editor
Charley Eatchel
Audrey Hoisington

Publisher
Sam Van Cook

Publishing Operations Manager
TaneshaNicole Kozler

Publishing Operations Assistant
Charley Eatchel

Social Media and Marketing
Isabelle Miller
Eric Tu

OTHER BOOKS BY BUTTON POETRY

If you enjoyed this book, please consider checking out some of our others, below. Readers like you allow us to keep broadcasting and publishing. Thank you!

Rachel Wiley, *Revenge Body*
Ebony Stewart, *BloodFresh*
Ebony Stewart, *Home.Girl.Hood.*
Kyle Tran Myhre, *Not A Lot of Reasons to Sing, but Enough*
Steven Willis, *A Peculiar People*
Topaz Winters, *So, Stranger*
Darius Simpson, *Never Catch Me*
Blythe Baird, *Sweet, Young, & Worried*
Siaara Freeman, *Urbanshee*
Robert Wood Lynn, *How to Maintain Eye Contact*
Junious 'Jay' Ward, *Composition*
Usman Hameedi, *Staying Right Here*
Sean Patrick Mulroy, *Hated for the Gods*
Sierra DeMulder, *Ephemera*
Taylor Mali, *Poetry By Chance*
Matt Coonan, *Toy Gun*
Matt Mason, *Rock Stars*
Miya Coleman, *Cottonmouth*
Ty Chapman, *Tartarus*
Lara Coley, *ex traction*
DeShara Suggs-Joe, *If My Flowers Bloom*
Ollie Schminkey, *Where I Dry the Flowers*
Edythe Rodriguez, *We, the Spirits*
Topaz Winters, *Portrait of My Body as a Crime I'm Still Committing*
Zach Goldberg, *I'd Rather Be Destroyed*
Eric Sirota, *The Rent Eats First*
Neil Hilborn, *About Time*
Josh Tvrdy, *Smut Psalm*
Phil SaintDenisSanchez, *before & after our bodies*
Ebony Stewart, *WASH*
L.E. Bowman, *Shapeshifter*
Najya Williams, *on a date with disappointment*
Jalen Eutsey, *Bubble Gum Stadium*
Meg Ford, *Wild/Hurt*
Jared Singer, *Forgotten Necessities*
Daniel Elias Galicia, *Still Desert*

Available at buttonpoetry.com/shop and more!

BUTTON POETRY BEST SELLERS

Neil Hilborn, *Our Numbered Days*
Hanif Abdurraqib, *The Crown Ain't Worth Much*
Olivia Gatwood, *New American Best Friend*
Sabrina Benaim, *Depression & Other Magic Tricks*
Melissa Lozada-Oliva, *peluda*
Rudy Francisco, *Helium*
Rachel Wiley, *Nothing Is Okay*
Neil Hilborn, *The Future*
Phil Kaye, *Date & Time*
Andrea Gibson, *Lord of the Butterflies*
Blythe Baird, *If My Body Could Speak*
Rudy Francisco, *I'll Fly Away*
Andrea Gibson, *You Better Be Lightning*
Rudy Francisco, *Excuse Me As I Kiss The Sky*

Available at buttonpoetry.com/shop and more!